The Life Cycle
of a
CROCODILE

By Barbara M. Linde

Gareth Stevens
Publishing

Please visit our Web site, www.garethstevens.com. For a free color catalog of all our high-quality books, call toll free 1-800-542-2595 or fax 1-877-542-2596.

Library of Congress Cataloging-in-Publication Data

Linde, Barbara M.
 The life cycle of a crocodile / Barbara M. Linde.
     p. cm. – (Nature's life cycles)
 Includes index.
 ISBN 978-1-4339-4672-1 (pbk.)
 ISBN 978-1-4339-4673-8 (6-pack)
 ISBN 978-1-4339-4671-4 (library binding)
 1. Crocodiles—Life cycles—Juvenile literature. I. Title.

  QL666.C925L56 2011
  597.98'2156–dc22

                                        2010029687

First Edition

Published in 2011 by
Gareth Stevens Publishing
111 East 14th Street, Suite 349
New York, NY 10003

Copyright © 2011 Gareth Stevens Publishing

Designer: Daniel Hosek
Editor: Therese Shea

Photo credits: Cover, pp. 1, 9 Fethi Belaid/AFP/Getty Images; pp. 4–5, 7, 21 (all images) Shutterstock.com; pp. 11, 15 Jonathan S. Blair/National Geographic/Getty Images; pp. 12–13 AFP/Getty Images; p. 17 Tal Cohen/AFP/Getty Images; p. 19 Roberto Schmidt/Getty Images.

Printed in the United States of America

CPSIA compliance information: Batch #CW11GS : For further information contact Gareth Stevens, New York, New York at 1-800-542-2595.

Contents

Words in the glossary appear in **bold** type the first time they are used in the text.

What Is a Crocodile?

A crocodile is a **reptile**. Its skin is covered with tough scales. It has a long, pointy **snout**. Some of its sharp, pointy teeth stick out when the crocodile closes its mouth.

Crocodiles have four short legs. They have five toes on each front foot. On each back foot, they have four **webbed** toes. A claw is at the end of each toe.

When a crocodile swims, it looks like the letter "S." Its rear legs go straight back. Its powerful tail moves back and forth.

▲
The skin on a crocodile's back is tough. The skin on its stomach is quite soft.

Where They Live

Crocodiles live in salt water or freshwater. They spend some time on land, so they like to stay near the shore. However, crocodiles can swim quite far.

Crocodiles live all over the world. There are 14 **species** of crocodiles. Some species live in just one place.

Crocodiles are cold-blooded. "Cold-blooded" means the **temperature** inside the body depends on the temperature outside the body. If the air is cold, the crocodile is cold. If the air is warm, the crocodile is warm.

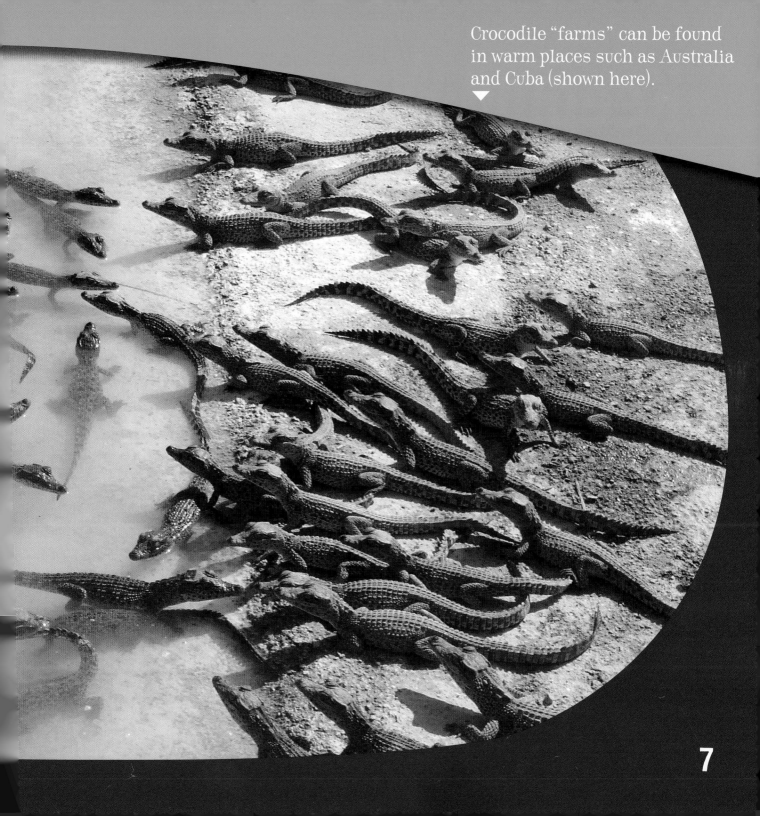

Crocodile "farms" can be found in warm places such as Australia and Cuba (shown here).

Keeping Warm

During hot months, the sun keeps crocodiles warm. When crocodiles get too hot, they swim.

In colder months, crocodiles dig dens near the water. They rest in them on the coldest days. On warmer days, they lay in the sun. They don't eat a lot when it's cold.

In spring, crocodiles become active again. They hunt for food. They also look for **mates**. Then, er crocodile gets ready to lay her eggs.

AWESOME ANIMAL!

Crocodiles can go without eating for months. They can live without food for a whole year if necessary!

A crocodile cools its brain by opening its mouth!

Eggs in the Nest

The mother crocodile makes a nest. Some mothers dig holes for their nests. Others build a mound of dirt and plants. The nest is near water, but not too close. She doesn't want her eggs to wash away!

After the nest is ready, the mother lays her eggs. A group of eggs is called a clutch. A clutch may have from 30 to 100 eggs. The eggs are white and have hard shells. The mother crocodile covers her clutch with plants. The plants help keep the eggs warm.

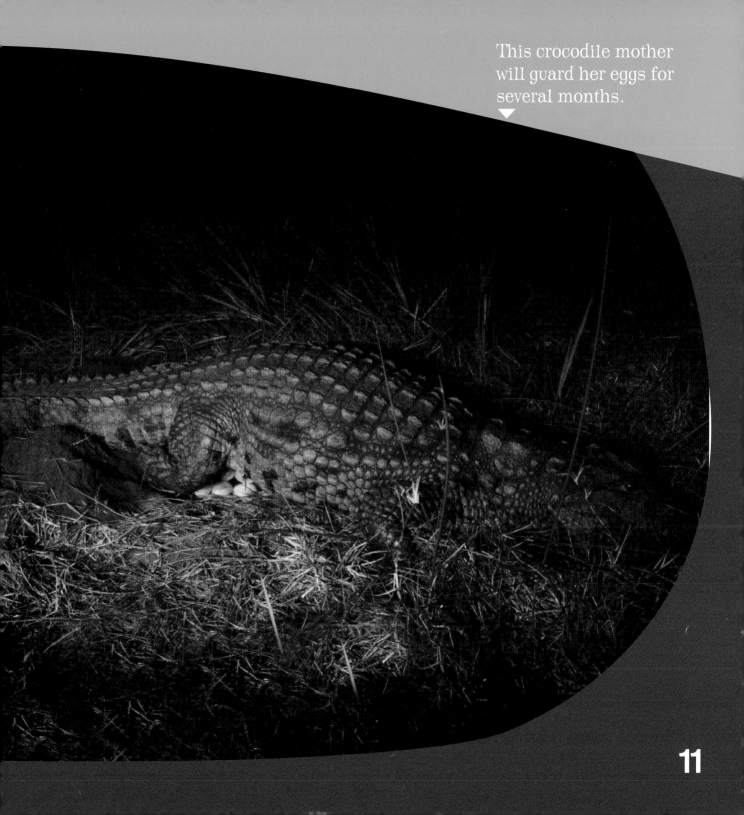

This crocodile mother will guard her eggs for several months.
▼

11

Breaking Out

The mother crocodile stays and guards her eggs. If an animal comes too close, she'll chase it away. Even the father crocodile stays back.

After 2 or 3 months, the eggs are ready to **hatch**. The babies make noises inside their eggs. The mother hears them. She uncovers the nest. Each baby crocodile has a pointy bump on its snout called an egg tooth. The baby uses its egg tooth to crack the tough shell.

AWESOME ANIMAL!

When a crocodile loses a tooth, a new one grows in. A crocodile may have over 1,000 teeth during its life!

Less than one out of four crocodile eggs hatch in the wild. Many are eaten first.
▼

Baby Crocodiles

If a baby has trouble breaking out of its egg, the mother crocodile rolls the egg around in her mouth. Finally, the shell cracks. The baby is free!

Now the mother opens her mouth very wide. All the babies crawl in. Carefully, the mother takes her babies to the water. She teaches them to swim. Sometimes the father crocodile helps, too.

Baby crocodiles are **prey** for other animals, such as snakes and snapping turtles. Most baby crocodiles don't live long.

This crocodile nest was found near the Nile River in Africa.

Young Crocodiles

Young crocodiles grunt or squeak to ask for help. The whole group stays together. Mostly they hunt in water that isn't very deep.

Young crocodiles stay with their mother up to a year. The youngsters grow about 1 foot (30 cm) in a year. They grow this quickly for the first 3 or 4 years. After that, their growth slows. Crocodiles begin to mate when they are about 10 years old.

AWESOME ANIMAL!

The ziczac bird eats bugs off crocodiles. The bird goes in and out of a crocodile's mouth without getting eaten!

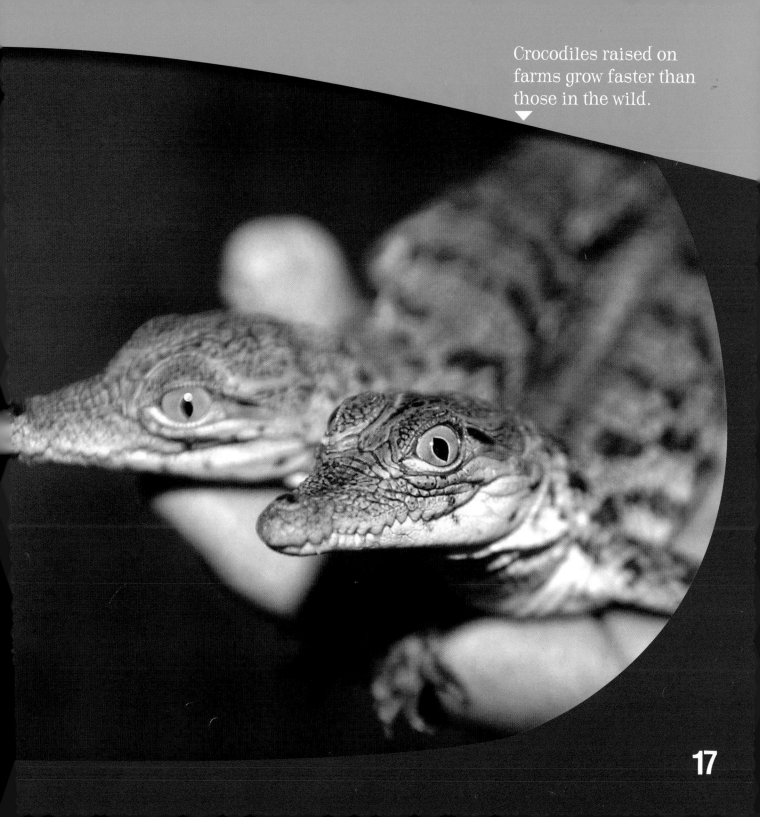

Crocodiles raised on farms grow faster than those in the wild.
▼

Adult Crocodiles

Some kinds of adult crocodiles are over 20 feet (6 m) long. They can live to be 80 years old. Adult crocodiles are **predators**. They eat birds, fish, and land animals such as deer, buffalo, and monkeys.

The crocodile hides in the water. Its eyes, ears, and the top of its snout peek out. It can hear, see, and smell from far away. It swims underwater to its prey. In a flash, it pulls the prey into the water. A crocodile may also knock an animal into the water with its tail.

AWESOME ANIMAL!

A crocodile can hold its breath for 8 hours in very cold water.

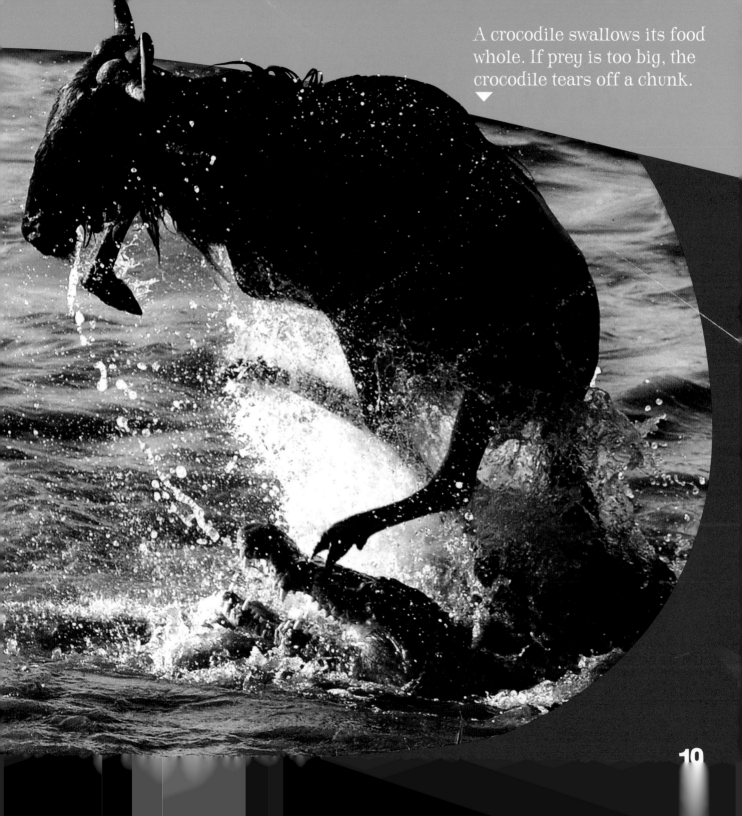

A crocodile swallows its food whole. If prey is too big, the crocodile tears off a chunk.

Crocodiles in Danger

Crocodiles lived on Earth before the dinosaurs! However, they're in danger of disappearing. In some places, people hunt crocodiles. They build houses and roads over the waters where crocodiles live.

Florida is the only U.S. state with crocodiles. In the 1970s, there were not many left. A law helped crocodile families grow.

There are special crocodile parks and farms. Some live in zoos or **aquariums**. Visitors can see these amazing animals during all parts of their life cycle.

The Life Cycle of a Crocodile

egg

baby crocodile

adult crocodile

young crocodile

Glossary

aquarium: a place to visit fish and other water animals

hatch: to come out of an egg

mate: an animal that comes together with another animal to make babies

predator: an animal that kills other animals for food

prey: an animal that is eaten by other animals

reptile: a cold-blooded animal with a backbone and scaly skin

snout: the mouth and nose of an animal

species: one kind of living thing. All people are one species.

temperature: how hot or cold something is

webbed: having thin skin between the toes

For More Information

Books

Bender, Lionel. *Crocodile*. North Mankato, MN: Smart Apple Media, 2005.

Pringle, Laurence. *Alligators and Crocodiles! Strange and Wonderful*. Honesdale, PA: Boyds Mills Press, 2009.

Tourville, Amanda Doering. *A Crocodile Grows Up*. Minneapolis, MN: Picture Window Books, 2007.

Web Sites

Crocodiles!

www.pbs.org/wgbh/nova/crocs/

The NOVA show's crocodile links include facts about how crocodiles outlasted the dinosaurs.

Nile Crocodiles

kids.nationalgeographic.com/kids/animals/creaturefeature/nile-crocodile/

Video, maps, facts, photos, and more are found on this National Geographic site.

Publisher's note to educators and parents: Our editors have carefully reviewed these Web sites to ensure that they are suitable for students. Many Web sites change frequently, however, and we cannot guarantee that a site's future contents will continue to meet our high standards of quality and educational value. Be advised that students should be closely supervised whenever they access the Internet.

Index